Sundays at 8am

Over Coffee is a weekly Sunday morning variety show where Rev. Dave Thompson listens to the spiritual stories of his guests. The show includes open mic peformances from various artists.

http://overcoffee.tv

Over Coffee

Over Coffee

Rev. Dave Thompson

Over Coffee is entirely a work of fiction. Nonetheless, some names and personal characteristics of individuals, places or events have been changed in order to disguise identities. Any resulting resemblance to persons, living or dead, or places or events is entirely coincidental and unintentional.

All Scripture quotations, unless otherwise indicated, are taken from the Holy Bible, New International Version®, NIV®, Copyright © 1973, 1978, 1984, 2011 by Biblica Inc.™

Copyright © 2014, 2015 Rev. Dave Thompson. All rights reserved.

Visit at revdavethompson.com

Published in the United States by World Uniting Press, a program of World Uniting, Intl'.

WORLD UNITING PRESS and colophon are registered trademarks of World Uniting, International.

Visit at worlduniting.org

No part of this publication may be reproduced, stored in a retrieval system, or transmitted, in any form, or by any means, electronic, mechanical, photocopying, recording, or otherwise, without the prior consent of the publisher.

Version 2.1

Library of Congress Cataloging-in-Publication Data
Thompson, Dave.
1st ed.
Over Coffee: a conversation for gay partnership and conservative faith / by Rev. Dave Thompson
p. cm.
ISBN 9780983567738 (Paperback) (alk. paper)
ISBN 9780983567769 (EPUB)
ISBN 9780983567776 (MOBI)
LCCN 2010929905
1. Gay--Social aspects. 2. Gay. 3. Christian.

Printed in the United States of America on acid-free paper. Print book and ebooks created using BookShop™.

To my family, thank you for being my first and my continuing refuge for love, learning, and limitless patience.

To my friends, thank you for your generosity, your tolerance, and your un-ending encouragement.

Table of Contents

A Pastor, an Author, and a Small-Town Cafe 1

What I am Not Arguing 21
    The Politics of Civil Marriage 23
    A Liberal Interpretation of Scripture 28

Defining Gay 31
    The 'Lifestyle' Myth 32
    Is He Truly Gay? 40

Conversion Therapy... Can You Fix Gay? 47
    Odd Man 'Out' 48
    Reparative Therapy and Fixing 'Gay' 52
    Puberty? Again?! 62
    Conversion or Suppression? 68

What About the Bible 73
    Literally Speaking 78
    God's Law vs God's Intention 79
    Priorities 81
    Commands, Context and Conflict 85

Jesus and Human Ability 91
    Gay Partnership: a Human Ability 99

Moving Forward: Obstacle or Opportunity? 105
    The Challenge of the Viewable 107

A New Education 109

Friendly Goodbyes 113

About the Author 117

Upcoming Works 0

Contact Info 119

Foreword

Walk into any bookstore and you will find droves of books concerning faith and being gay. The vast majority have joined the ranks, siding up in the battle, authors following suit by writing yet another take on why the other side is wrong, misguided, or even evil.

So it was refreshing to read Dave's book. Rather than an argument, Dave presents a conversation. Rather than waging a war over a battlefield, Dave presents a give-and-take over coffee. The narrative, set between himself and a small-town pastor is a quick read. I found myself easily engrossed, sitting with the characters at the coffee house table, listening to and enjoying a refreshingly real, graceful, and honest conversation between very real people, circumstances, and biblical faith. I was surprised to witness a subtle give and take across what has often been an un-traversable chasm of hostility.

One of the more unexpected elements of the conversation was the manner in which Dave was able to reposition the gay issue alongside of everything else that is often considered as understandable human circumstance in the Church. In fact, there was nothing really unorthodox, or new about his position. Instead, I found a refreshing return to a gospel of pragmatic grace, including gay persons along with everyone else, providing them, as we do with other people with complicated circumstances, the means to enable the greatest ideal of relationship matching the reality of their unalterable state.

I am excited to see a fellow Christian and also a fellow musician who, having served in conservative pastoral roles, has not been willing to forego his convictions of faith. In the light of those who may disagree, Dave continues to bring a message of grace, not just for the comfort of those who more easily fit a presumed standard, but for those whom Jesus kept company with, the unlikely, the un-assumed, and the unwelcome.

Jason Warner of Jason & deMarco

Author's Note

It was after a three hour conversation over coffee with a favorite pastor friend of mine, that I considered writing this work for the first time. A married and devoted man, he has been friends since college and at seminary and is one of the most remarkable Christians I have met to this day. He is without question a shining example of biblical faith extending true and practical love while demonstrating an innate ability for remarkable academic scholarship.

When he said he would consider allowing gay, partnered persons to be members of the church he pastored, under the circumstances I laid out, I knew that I had to construct my dialogue more completely and present it as a written work for others to consider.

I have attempted to compose this narrative as near as possible to the actual conversations I have had and the very real circumstances that I or others have experienced. At times they are no doubt filtered through my own lens of recollection. However, my intent was to provide as realistic of a setting and conversation as possible, portraying the questions, reflections and responses as close as possible to my own experiences in conversations with pastors and people in or from a biblical faith.

The pastoral character in this story was pulled mainly from another close pastoral friend who has exhibited some of the most astonishing examples of sincere honesty, demonstrating unhindered human compassion and even more remarkably, a willingness to place the Scriptures above his own presumption, cultural paradigms, and denominational positions.

The main character John is built off of many of my own personal experiences. These circumstances are not uncommon to a number of men and women, many who still reside in our churches, as well as many, sadly, who have felt obligated, or who have been forced to leave our churches.

It was also my hope with this work to provide a unique perspective into the position of our brothers and sisters who might be labeled *conservative*, relating them as individuals of faith who are loving, compassionate and willing, but who are however unable to find a way to reconcile their biblical understanding with the acceptance of gay, partnered people as members in the church.

I would like to add that whereas this narrative is written utilizing the example of a gay man, I am hopeful that the discussion will find equal consideration among the many gay women in our congregations.

I would also like to thank my editors, Erin Peterson, Günther Bially and Kortney Thoma, who so graciously donated their time and provided some of the most thoughtful and honest reflection from their own experiences and expertise.

Last I would like to thank Pat and Chad, the owners and operators at their Old Milwaukee Cafe. They provided me a lovely spot to set this intimate conversation. They have both been very generous in their support of LGBT persons.

Chapter 1

A Pastor, an Author, and a Small–Town Cafe

Over Coffee

It was the kind of picturesque place that would come to mind if someone said 'small-town cafe.' The pastor was right, I would have been lost without his directions and I was relieved to see that I had arrived. I was encouraged to see the pastor at the front door of the Old Milwaukee Cafe. I waved and parked my car along the side of the road.

It was pouring rain outside, so I threw my jacket on and made a mad dash to the covered porch.

The small-town Washington pastor held the door open, shouting my name in a confiding manner, "Dave, I presume?!"

"So far," I replied, extended my hand, shouting back, "Pastor?!"

"Until they kick me out!" he hollered, gripping my hand in an over-zealous vice lock. I returned his

A Pastor, an Author, and a Small–Town Cafe

handshake with equal vigor, smiling. We entered the cafe and stood in the entry-way dripping as we began looking for a place to sit.

The pastor nodded familiarly at the nearby waitress, shouting "Mornin' Pat."

Pat came over, a plate of pancakes in hand, asking, "Where will it be Pastor, your usual?" He gave her another subtle nod, at which she jeered, "Wonderful, I already rolled out the white linens for ya!" en route to an eager table of ladies sipping their coffee.

I followed the pastor back to a table in the very back of the diner. I thought to myself—a smart place for a pastor to bring people; a low-key place where they could feel free to talk with some amount of privacy.

I eyeballed the menu and picked out the ham & eggs, which happened to be my favorite. It always reminded me of breakfast at my grandmother's house. My mind drifted quickly to the memory of her scolding me for putting ketchup on my eggs. A daughter of the Great Depression, she was constant in her reminder to be grateful for the simple things in life, and to enjoy contentment with what God had given, without the need for embellishment.

Pat came over with some coffee. I turned over my cup, excited to get some brew in me after waking up so early to join the pastor for coffee. She took my order and then looked over to the pastor who murmured, "the usual," followed by, "wheat toast today."

After a few seconds treating our coffee, the pastor opened, asking, "So are you from the city?"

I smiled, realizing what he was *really* asking. It was one of those let's-get-to-the-bottom-of-who-you-are questions. And it was often a nice way of saying, "you should probably realize: if you are a city-boy, you really aren't going to have much of a clue what life is like here, but I'll listen politely."

A Pastor, an Author, and a Small–Town Cafe

I replied, "Well, I've lived in a handful of places all over the country: eight states by current count, I believe. I spent my early years in a small lumber town in Oregon. But all in all I consider myself to be from Montana, since most of my formative years were spent there. I lived in Missoula."

"Ah, Missoula! So you're a fly-fisherman?!" he exclaimed, a quick reference, I thought, to the popular movie, *A River Runs Through It.* It was an adaptation of Norman Maclean's short story which most Montanans saw as a sort of two-edged sword. On the one hand most of us recognized the benefit to tourism, on the other hand, the very lonely rivers we grew up loving were now littered with so called "anglers" every twenty yards or so, casting their never-to-be-used-again fishing tackle at our now apathetic waters. For whatever reason, the Washington rivers had escaped the notice of the would-be outdoorsmen, for which I was very grateful.

I lifted my hand as if to testify, stating, "Well, my father certainly made sure we knew how to fish. Regrettably, I've only recently been back on the rivers. Thankfully I have begun to discover some

Over Coffee

very nice spots in western Washington. I have to say that there is something refreshing about standing in a river in the middle of God's creation and casting a line."

"Montana has some nice hunting too, I'd imagine." He added.

"The best in the world, to be sure." I paused for a moment thinking back. "Funny thing, I knew how to put meat on the table before I knew how to drive. That was the way of things there. Hunting was its own rite of passage. In fact the age of 12 was a big age. It meant that I could take my 'Hunter's Safety' course and finally have a license of my own. Even so, I had spent a handful of years shadowing my dad through the woods and snow long before that point."

"And you?" I asked, anxious to hear a bit more about him.

A Pastor, an Author, and a Small-Town Cafe

"Well, I haven't done much of anything the last couple of years. I've been pretty busy, but I'm hoping to get out and at least put my line on a couple of rivers this summer," he remarked with a tone of anticipation.

He continued, changing the subject a bit, "I read that you studied to be a Pentecostal preacher."

"Well, my First Communion and Confirmation were in the Roman Catholic Church, but yes, I studied to be a minister at a small Assemblies of God school, Trinity Bible College in North Dakota. But I finished my ministerial degree out here in Washington at Northwest University, affiliated with the same denomination."

"But you decided not to go into the ministry?" he asked, a bit perplexed.

"Well…" I started, not sure of how to explain, "there was a lot that I needed to work out before I felt I could take on a role of such significance."

Over Coffee

I added, "As Charles Spurgeon is often quoted as saying, 'If you are called to pastor, don't stoop to be called a king.'"

He smiled, nodding a bit and staring at the table as if looking into a deep pool of memories.

Pat came over with some coffee, putting one hand on her hip, remarking, "You boys are already through your first cup? I better get both pots going."

The pastor stirred his coffee a bit then continued, asking, "So what are you working on these days?"

I finished adding a generous portion of cream and sugar to the dark brew, answering, "Well, most recently I have been working on some new book projects, but primarily I've been speaking about my current book."

A Pastor, an Author, and a Small–Town Cafe

"Is that the book where you are talking about gay partnership in the Church?" he asked hurriedly.

"Yup, the very one."

"Well, that will provide a nice segue," he bemused.

"Oh? How's that?" I asked.

"I was hoping to hear your reflection on a situation that has come up in my congregation."

"Of course. I'm all ears." I settled in, ready to listen.

"So..." he began, giving a quick glance away from our table. I leaned in as he continued, "I've been working with a guy in my congregation who told me he was gay." He stated his words tentatively, followed by a pause, testing the waters for some type of change in my demeanor.

"Just recently?" I asked inquisitively.

"No this was a little ways back," he noted.

I questioned further, "How did he end up telling you?"

"He's always been the type to stop by the office and just sort of pop his head in and say hello. Most of the time it's just a friendly stop. You know, the sort of 'Howdy, Pastor,' that I get from many of my congregation members. I've always kept my door open so the congregation never feels like I am unreachable," he said with an air of pride. "But this one particular day, Dav..." he caught himself, stopping to cut short the man's name, "...John, seemed anxious."

A Pastor, an Author, and a Small–Town Cafe

"So what happened with...*John*." I asked, with a slight emphasis to his name so as to note that I was fine using a ghost-name for the point of our conversation and for the man's privacy.

Relieved, he continued, "Like I said, he was in a peculiar mood. I tried to do what I could to put him at ease, asking how his day was going. He just retorted with a distracted, 'Fine, oh, you know, busy as usual.'"

"He stood inside the doorway, glancing over my bookshelf, hands in his oversized Carhartts. Hoping to bring him a bit closer to his intention of being there, I asked him if he would like to have a seat. He asked me if he could close the door for a second. I told him that it would be fine."

"'Is everything OK?' I asked. 'You seem a bit distracted.'"

"He made his way over to the chair next to me, sort of scuttling along like a kid called into the

Over Coffee

principal's office. John is a big guy, not obese, just big...tall. As he sat down beside me I couldn't help but to feel a bit dwarfed in his shadow."

"So what happened?" I asked, drawn into the story.

"It was remarkable, Dave," the pastor added, holding his hands out to emphasize his point, "he changed in that moment. This towering, confident man seemed different. I could have sworn, for just a moment, I was looking back in time, at little Johnny, who had sat in that seat as a child years ago."

He shifted his weight quickly and continued, "He paused for a little while and said, 'Pastor, I need to tell you something, but I'm worried about what you'll think of me,'" he said with a pause.

Looking up at me, the pastor said, "I quickly changed my tone from camaraderie to concern. I couldn't imagine what he was going to say. I wheeled my chair a bit closer and reassured him,

A Pastor, an Author, and a Small-Town Cafe

'John, there is nothing that you can tell me that is going to change the fact that I consider you as much a son as a brother.'"

"I saw his uneasiness and asked him a bit more intently 'What's wrong?'"

"Tears began to well up in his eyes as I sat there waiting. Composing himself the best he could, he managed to say three words. 'Pastor...' he started, holding his breath back attempting to manage himself, 'I'm...gay.' Just as soon as he finished, he began to choke up and..."

The pastor ended his sentence abruptly, holding back his own breath, shocked a bit at his own emotional response.

I waited for a little while for the pastor to gain his composure, taking a couple of sips of my coffee.

"What did you do?" I finally asked.

Over Coffee

The pastor looked up at me, eyes still watery, "I did what any pastor should do!" he stated emphatically. "I wheeled my chair over beside him and put my arm around him." He paused, looking down at the table, then quietly added, "and we just sat there and cried together for a while."

The pastor turned his attention back to his cup of coffee, all the while looking intently into the steam. He was wrestling in a state of cherished recollection, holding the memory like a father would hold his injured son.

I paused for a moment, feeling my heart sink with empathy as I witnessed the pain in the pastor's eyes. Would that I could find more pastors with the wisdom and compassion to extend such understanding and love.

"Pastor," I murmured after a short time, "I hope you realize how incredibly fortunate John is to have you as his pastor. I am more accustomed to hearing rejection, insecurity and judgment in that type of situation."

A Pastor, an Author, and a Small–Town Cafe

"It seemed like the only thing I could do," he said with an air of helplessness.

Pat slowly approached with our orders, hesitant as she noticed the pastor's demeanor. "I've got your breakfast for you, Pastor." She smiled at me, placing the plates quickly in front of us and walking away in an attempt to belay the awkwardness.

We attended to our food and after a few minutes the pastor was in a place where he seemed to be able to talk.

"How did you move the conversation forward?" I asked out of pure curiosity.

"I asked him what type of guy he was attracted to," he admitted with a smile.

I laughed out loud, as did the pastor, welcoming the change in tone. I noted, "That was brave of you."

Over Coffee

"Well, I figured his experience in life was just as human as my own. I am attracted to certain types of women, so I figured he would be the same, but just directed to certain types of men."

"Again, pastor, you are a man of rare empathy. So, is that the situation you were speaking of?" I concluded.

"Well, not entirely. There's more." He continued, "We have been meeting together for a while. It has frankly been more about me asking him questions and getting to know this part of his life that I had never known."

"A few weeks ago he came to my office, as he has done fairly regularly since. He explained that he had been dating a guy who attends another church in the area. He told me that he wanted to make their relationship more substantial and suggested to me that they both wanted to be partnered. In his words,"

A Pastor, an Author, and a Small–Town Cafe

> Pastor, I love the Lord and I love this Church, but I love this man too, just as you love your wife. It's different, but the emotions are the same, and my desire to be partnered is just as strong as yours. I don't want to leave the church, but I don't want to be alone anymore. It's killing me, and I am not able to change that I'm gay.

"Wow," I retorted.

"I know," He agreed.

"That's a whole lot to consider. So what did you say?"

"I didn't know what to say. I couldn't deny his feelings. But I don't really have any way to provide room on the pew for that kind of relationship. I have not found any biblical way to allow it. And if I ever wanted to allow it, the congregation would need to have a pretty substantial argument."

Over Coffee

He confessed, "I was just honest with him. I told him that I understood what he was saying and that I couldn't imagine how hard it would be to have no option but to be single. I explained that I wanted to take some time to think and pray about this before I was prepared to give him an answer."

He took a deep breath, adding, "This is certainly not an easy issue to deal with."

"Welcome to my predicament," I smiled.

"I tried to do some research and really wanted to find some path for him. But there is just no possibility for him in all of the conservative materials I have been given by my governing district. I even looked at some materials that promote gay partnership in the Church. But they all seemed to require me to forsake my beliefs in Scripture, and for lack of a better term, become a liberal," he shuttered.

"God forbid!" I remarked sarcastically, taking a sip of coffee.

A Pastor, an Author, and a Small–Town Cafe

"God forbid!" The pastor echoed, smiling.

I continued, "So tell me a bit more about John. Is he from the area? Were you aware of his orientation prior to this?"

"No." he said with an emphasis of shock. "I didn't know he was gay. He was practically born on the pew of our Church. I've known him since he was in diapers. All of his family have been committed members of the Church, serving in all kinds of programs. His parents were missionaries for a time and his dad served on the board. In fact, his dad has been my doctor ever since I moved here; a good man, as far as they come."

"Honestly, I didn't see that one coming. I know he dated a gal in high school, and he was near engaged to a gal in college, but hasn't really dated since then. I think most of us just chalked it up to the fact that he was a really quality guy and was being overly picky about the kind of gal he dated. He also runs a pretty successful business in town so I

Over Coffee

figured he was probably too busy to date. So no, he never really made it very obvious."

He added, with a bit of remorse, "You know, in some ways I think it bothered me a bit to think that someone I cared about so much had something so substantial that they felt they could not share with me, that I've known for so many years."

"I can't imagine it was easy for him to tell you," I sympathized.

"No, I don't suppose I have made it very easy to talk about either. I have never been very vocal on the gay issue from the pulpit. I guess I thought that not talking about it would make it easier for people to deal with. As it turns out, not talking about it didn't work either."

"True, silence can often be interpreted as a taboo," I concurred.

Chapter 2
What I Am Not Arguing

Over Coffee

The Pastor continued, "I talked with a close ministerial friend of mine about this whole ordeal and he mentioned what you were working on. He also mentioned that you studied to be a Pentecostal minister, which piqued my interest. So...I guess you're arguing a biblical case for gay marriage?"

"Well, not exactly," I began.

"So what *are* you arguing," he inquired.

"I should probably start with what I am *not* arguing."

"Uh oh, a politician," he teased.

"No, just someone who is trying to be careful about a loaded issue in an area riddled with a number of landmines," I remarked with a smile.

What I Am Not Arguing

He let out a single laugh, adding, "That's probably wise."

The Politics of Civil Marriage

"First let me note that my conversation is intended specifically for the Church, rather than the general population, or *secular* audiences. I am only speaking to the sacrament, or biblical teaching of marriage and not at all to the politics of civil, legal and economic marriage."

I continued, "So in our Church context I should note that I am not arguing that the sacrament of marriage as we have structured it, should simply include gay partnerships into the exact same model. A union between opposite genders is different than a union between same genders. Also, the joining of a man and a woman seems to be a uniquely intended union in God's creative work."

I paused, and asked, "I hope you don't mind me quickly running through the Creation saga with you. I realize that this is old hat, but I hope you'll indulge me for the sake of being able to lay the foundation for what I'm suggesting."

"Not at all," he replied, slightly amused.

I began again, "Within a conservative interpretation of Scripture, the Creation story seems very clear concerning the intention of God splitting us into woman and man. As Genesis informs us, we were initially a single, genderless creature. God gave His first commandment, to Himself, that it wasn't good for His creature to be alone. We needed a relationship. It was our need for companionship that drove God to separate us into two genders. So it seems fairly clear what God's intention was: that which was separated, was meant to be joined back together as one flesh, able to commune with each other in a unique way."

I continued, "God then gave His second commandment, the first to us, that we should be fruitful and multiply. So there is something uniquely intended, special and essential about the intimate

What I Am Not Arguing

union of a man and a woman, who were pulled apart, specifically for the other's relationship."

"So you don't believe in gay marriage?" he asked, confused.

I clarified, "For this work, I am only talking within the context of the Church and not in the context of civil law. The civic, economic, and legal contract of marriage, which unfortunately holds the same name as our sacrament, is a matter for another work altogether."

"So you're not talking about marriage."

"Not in the civil sense."

"Is that your next book?" he asked, smiling.

"It certainly is a subject that needs to be discussed. We as Christians are challenged to somehow live within two contracts: our *faith* contract with God and our *social* contract with our country. Naturally we are compelled to obey our faith contract first. Still, we live with people of many different beliefs who also pay taxes and vote. We depend on them as much as they depend on us for our mutual economy, law, and liberties. We must extend to them the same liberties and benefits we ourselves enjoy in our social contract *and* we must afford to them the same freedom of religion that we ourselves enjoy. Before the law, we should all be treated equally. All that to say, for the purpose of our faith contract, I'm only conversing about the partnering of two gay Christians together in the Church at this point."

"Why the distinction?" he asked.

"Good question. I should clarify that I am using the term marriage to describe, as the early Church patriarch, Augustine of Hippo defines sacrament, "a visible sign of an invisible reality.""

I continued, "In the church we provide a ceremony and ritual around marriage between a man

What I Am Not Arguing

and a woman so as to provide a visible sign of what God has brought together. As the New Testament author, Matthew, in quoting Jesus writes,"

> "Haven't you read," he replied, "that at the beginning the Creator 'made them male and female,' and said, 'For this reason a man will leave his father and mother and be united to his wife, and the two will become one flesh'? So they are no longer two, but one. Therefore what God has joined together, let man not separate."
>
> - Matt 19:4-6 NIV

I added, "Whether or not we as Christians support gay marriage within our *social* contract, I am suggesting that at very least it is biblical and necessary for us to allow two gay people to share their life together in an open and affirming manner in our Church communities."

The pastor paused for a moment, then responded, "Well, I wasn't expecting you to sidestep the politics of marriage. I guess I'm just used to the 'agenda' being only about the politics of gay marriage. I have to say, I appreciate you making a distinction between what we believe concerning the doctrine of marriage in our Churches, and what we decide socially concerning legal and civil marriage."

A Liberal Interpretation of Scripture

"Second, I am not asking my fellow believers to give up their convictions concerning the Word of God. I believe the Bible is inspired by God."

"So what *are* you arguing for?" he chuckled.

"Well, the long and short of it is that I am presenting the case for repositioning gay partnership alongside all of the other human circumstances we welcome in our churches. I am arguing the case for allowing two gay Christians, who are unable

What I Am Not Arguing

to change their orientation, who do not desire nor possess a gift to be celibate, and who desire to live by the same teachings as all other Christians, to be partnered together. This provides the means for them to be able to keep God's first commandment, that His creature should not be alone, and so fulfill the intention of the Law."

Over Coffee

# Chapter 3
Defining 'Gay'

Over Coffee

Pat came over to our table, asking if we wanted more coffee. The pastor nodded, saying, "Decaf, please."

Pat grinned and said, "I'm going to bring you boys a carafe of coffee. The way you are both drinking it down, you'd think you were solving the world's problems."

The 'Lifestyle' Myth

The pastor took a few sips of coffee and then looked up at me hesitantly. I raised my eyebrows, to show that I was waiting for his question.

He began, "I have to be honest with you. I have a tough time seeing the gay culture as being anything but counter-Christian."

"How is that?" I questioned.

Defining 'Gay'

"I watch the news...some hardly seem to live lives that would be considered Christian."

"Ri-ight, because the news always paints an accurate picture and never serves up hasty generalizations of different groups," I joked. "So, how do you mean?"

He drew an imaginary circle on the table with his finger, saying "Well, take for instance gay bars. I understand that they are a place where people go to 'hook-up,'" using finger-quotes as emphasis. He continued, "In the reading I've done, there are a number of ex-gay guys who claimed that when they were in the lifestyle, they were going to bars and hooking up with other guys."

I shrugged my shoulders a bit, "Well, that sounds to me like these ex-gay guys had a problem with their own lifestyle; more of a personal problem than it being a gay issue in general. It sounds like these guys had some difficulty managing their behavior, particularly when it came to promiscuity."

Over Coffee

"You don't think that that is the gay lifestyle?" He asked, confused.

"Have you heard of a book called *A Place at the Table*?" I asked.

"No," he admitted.

"The author, Bruce Bawer, makes a very strong assertion that many people who consider themselves gay do not go to bars. Many find the idea of hooking-up to be completely undesirable to them and their ideals. Unfortunately for the gay community, generally speaking, these people blend into society as a whole since there is nothing obvious to distinguish them as being gay."

I continued, "It is pretty difficult to find anything mentioned about that in the more conservative literature. On the contrary, I personally know many gay people who do not prefer that type of lifestyle at all."

Defining 'Gay'

The pastor reflected, "Come to think of it, I haven't seen anything like that in the more conservative literature I've read either."

"Pastor, can I ask you a question?" I inquired.

"Of course," he asserted.

"As a pastor, have you ever had to deal with *straight* people who are substance abusers, or who hook-up with other people in a promiscuous manner?"

"Not as much with the members of our church, thank goodness, but I certainly have had to counsel couples who needed help dealing with infidelity. It's in my dealings within the community that I typically see more openly promiscuous lifestyles."

"So it would seem that alcoholism, substance abuse and promiscuity are more of a human concern than a gay one, wouldn't you agree?" I pressed.

"Yes, I suppose that is true." He offered a conceding nod.

"In fact, I'm pretty sure that Alcoholics Anonymous has just as many, if not more, straight members than gay ones."

"Well, that is certainly true," he affirmed.

"And consider what it must be like as a gay social group to have no social structure or support to encourage them to live a life that the Church would consider beneficial."

The pastor sat back in his seat a bit in contemplation, noting, "I suppose there isn't really any place for them to go that would provide that sort of ready-made social framework, especially since they don't likely feel very welcome in the Church."

Defining 'Gay'

"And let's take the example of John. I find it interesting that the one gay person that you know hardly seems to fit the bill, wouldn't you agree?"

The pastor smiled, "No, he certainly doesn't. In fact, we've talked a bit about that. He told me that he had been to a couple of gay bars but didn't really find them to be very interesting. He said that he made a couple of friends here and there, but since he didn't drink he found it easier to get to know other gay guys over coffee. He actually joined a group that provided hiking activities for gay people, so evidently he's found some friends there."

"It's a shame that they can't meet at Church," I stated.

The pastor shrugged, noting, "I suppose. The guy that John is hoping to partner with is one he met at a support group for gay Christians."

The pastor thought for a second and continued, "I think most only see gay people as those who are marching in the street with signs; yelling and generally just angry. Or they are marching in parades, in costume, or some other very revealing clothing."

He tilted his head forward and raised his eyebrows, saying, "John said that he never really felt comfortable with that type of thing."

"I certainly can understand his lack of identification. Though I also understand that many of those people are helping to promote the awareness of their perspective, just as much as I see the more conservative groups voicing themselves in a similar fashion; well... with more clothes on," I laughed.

Continuing, I said, "I think many gay people probably have the same perspective of the Conservative Church. For the most part they also only see the ones who are in parades, carrying signs and often with an angry demeanor."

Defining 'Gay'

The pastor nodded. "I'm sure that is the case. Though I wish they could see so many of the good, loving and caring people that I know."

"I'm sure they would say the same," I reflected.

The pastor continued his questioning. "So what do you do with the claim that gay people are promiscuous and incapable of having a monogamous relationship?"

I quickly retorted, "The same thing I do with the claim that straight people are promiscuous and incapable of having a monogamous relationship. I would say there are those people. But I'm guessing that I don't have to spend too much time pointing out that straight people are faced with the same human tendencies. In fact, I personally know three or four straight people off the top of my head who live openly promiscuous lives and recreationally use drugs/alcohol. And I'm sure that you'd agree that straight people don't have the corner on the market for monogamous relationships."

Over Coffee

"I suppose that is fair," he conceded.

I added, "I can, however, point out a number of gay people that I know who don't use drugs, won't touch alcohol, don't go to bars, and are committed to their partners monogamously. They have been able to do all of this despite society, churches and often families inferring and expecting them to be unable to accomplish this."

Is He Truly Gay?

The pastor finished studying his coffee, took a sip and glanced over with a bit of a helpless stare, as if baiting me to lead the conversation a bit.

I did, asking, "This may sound like a strange question: do you think John is purely gay?"

"Well, he wants to be with a guy, so...." he witted.

Defining 'Gay'

I clarified, "What I mean is, is he a true 'Kinsey five or six,' or do you think he is somewhere else on the scale?"

"What scale?" he asked, puzzled.

"Forgive me. Are you familiar with the 'Kinsey Scale?'"

"Can't say that I am."

I explained, "Back in the 1940's, during one of the more conservative times in our nation, Dr. Alfred Kinsey conducted some of the most academic research ever published on human sexuality. He wrote a book, Sexual Behavior in the Human Male, where he creates a scale from zero to six concerning the sexual orientation of the human male. A zero represented those who identified as exclusively heterosexual and a six represented those who identified as exclusively homosexual."

Over Coffee

"His research discovered that there were men spread across the entire spectrum. 50% of the male population was found to be exclusively heterosexual throughout their adult lives, whereas four percent were exclusively homosexual."

The pastor noted, "I've never heard that. And the other numbers?"

"The remaining 46% were spread fairly evenly between different combinations of both orientations," I added.

"Interesting..." he remarked staring down at his coffee in a thoughtful manner. He finally continued, "I know that I've often heard gay advocates say that ten percent of the population is gay. But then on the conservative side they try to put the percentage at more like one or two percent."

I nodded. "I'm not really sure that it matters all that much. At least both sides agree that there are people who are truly gay. I don't even think it takes

Defining 'Gay'

statistical analysis to discover that there are in fact gay people."

"No, I don't suppose it does. The fact of the matter is that I have a gay member in my congregation."

After a few moments, continuing to stare at his coffee he remarked, in a somber tone, "I've been in the ministry a long time now. I'd wish I could say it is as easy as gay and straight, but even I have to acknowledge the reality of what I know of my own congregation. The majority appear to be normal, I mean straight...sorry" he interjected, "I mean straight. But I know of a few other folks who have expressed concerns that they might be gay. When they told me, I just offered my own reflection and experience, that it was not unusual for people to have those curiosities at times. So, this Kinsey scale would pretty well reflect my own experience."

I paused for a moment, refreshed to hear such an honest statement. I couldn't help but to say, "I wish that more pastors had the insight that you do and the brave soul to be honest about what they observe."

The pastor replied, "I wish I could call it insight, or even bravery. I'm just calling it like it is. It's not going to help anyone to be dishonest. And either way, God is still forced to deal with our realities, even if we want to brush them under the carpet and cover them with furniture."

He continued, saying "I certainly have not done as much research as you have on the subject; but in all of the material available to me, I never came across a Kinsey Scale, or anything resembling it."

"That's understandable," I acknowledged. "In all of my early study coming from a conservative Christian perspective and using their materials I rarely found anything mentioning it. But I suppose that it makes sense; it's easier to deal with people in black and white categories."

Defining 'Gay'

I restated my question, "So what do you think about John? Is he a Kinsey five or six?"

"He did mention that he has never had any attraction to a woman at any time in his life. So I suppose he might be a Kinsey six. I guess I'm confused at why you feel the distinction is important."

I clarified, "Well, the case that I'm presenting presumes that both gay persons who want to be partnered are truly Kinsey sixes, or even Kinsey fives who have only been incidentally heterosexual, but aren't actually oriented to the opposite sex."

"Why is that important?"

"Well in the case of a Kinsey zero through four, there exists some manner of straight orientation. In this situation it might be possible for them to favor a relationship with the opposite sex."

Over Coffee

The pastor interjected, "So if John is a Kinsey five or six, you think he will not be able to change?"

I explained, "I think it is less about change than it is about being able to favor an orientation that is already available."

The pastor thought to himself, then noted, "I'd have to ask John to clarify, but I think he would consider himself a Kinsey five or six. He doesn't seem to have ever had any attraction to women."

I specified, "I should probably clarify that for the sake of what I am presenting, I am using the term 'gay' to represent those who are Kinsey fives or sixes, or who do not possess an orientation to the opposite sex. So in the case of gay partnership, John would be in that category. He only possesses an orientation to the same sex."

Chapter 4

Conversion Therapy...Can You Fix 'Gay?'

Over Coffee

Odd Man 'Out'

In an effort to find out a little more about John, I asked, "So how much have you talked with John about his being gay?"

"We've spent a number of months talking about it."

"Has he ever talked about trying to change his orientation?"

"Yes, as a matter of fact he attended a ministry for changing gay people, called Exodus or something... " he trailed off.

"Exodus International?"

"Yes, I think that was it," he concurred.

Conversion Therapy...Can You Fix 'Gay?'

"I'm guessing he was not successful?"

"He said that he did everything that he could, but has had no success. Evidently, he has been trying for years, ever since he was in high school."

"That's certainly not unusual," I reflected.

The pastor shifted his weight, "I guess, but I'm a bit confused. I have tried to spend as much time as I can, researching these groups, and they claim to have a handful of success cases. I don't really know John to be dishonest. He's always been the type of person to just get stuff done. In fact, I put him in charge of the beautification committee for the Church and in four months we ended up with a new roof and a porch for the church. But I suppose he has to be that way, or his business would not be as successful as it is."

The pastor continued his reflection, "It's hard to believe that if he put an effort into it, it wouldn't work, unless it just isn't able to be done. But then, my denominational higher-ups keep telling me that it's something that can change, since it's just a behavior. They keep saying that it's not an acceptable lifestyle. I guess I understand their perspective on the gay lifestyle," he qualified, "but John's not at all like a lot of the gay people you see on TV."

"What do you mean?" I asked, curious.

"Well, as I said before, he's not the type to march in parades, or hold up angry signs, or scream and yell."

"You mean, he's not a conservative fundamentalist Christian?" I jabbed.

"Touché." He laughed. "So sad that is what we have become known for."

"I agree."

Conversion Therapy...Can You Fix 'Gay?'

"I mean, there are a lot of wonderful people in my church who are kind as the day is long," he said, almost pleadingly.

"I feel the same. But they don't make the evening news, I'm afraid."

He took a deep breath. "Anyway, I just mean to say that John doesn't really fit the kind of lifestyle that most of my leadership are talking about."

I agreed with him, noting, "Unfortunately, it's often the same for many other gay people. I personally know a number of men and women who are gay and you would never know it. They are just people who are trying to make their way in this world. Many of them are, more remarkably still, practicing Christians, though they are not allowed to worship in the conservative churches that many of them called home."

Over Coffee

Reparative Therapy and Fixing 'Gay'

The pastor turned to a new question, "I was directed by my District Superintendent to go to a website that dealt with helping gay people change their orientation. I have spent quite a bit of time reading their material, though probably not as much as you have. Have you seen the website 'narth.com?'"

"Yes, of course, NARTH, the National Association for Research & Therapy of Homosexuality. I am very familiar with it." I replied.

"They seem to promote that gay people can and should leave the gay lifestyle and change."

"Yes, that is their perspective, though I'm still not sure what lifestyle they are referring to. It seems to me that John, for example, lives a life that is hardly different than anyone else. In fact his lifestyle seems to be head-and-shoulders above most straight people," I smiled.

Conversion Therapy...Can You Fix 'Gay?'

"I think they mean his choice of sexual orientation. He should choose a straight orientation, rather than choosing a gay one," he stated.

"Hmmm... may I ask you a question?"

"Sure." He took a sip of coffee.

"When did you choose your straight orientation?"

"Me?!" He chuckled a bit adding, "I've only ever been attracted to women. I was never attracted to men so there was no choice in the matter."

"So why would that be any different for John? I would imagine that he would agree he was simply never attracted to women and only ever attracted to men."

I continued, "Do you think you could successfully be converted to being attracted to men?"

Over Coffee

He laughed, "Not likely."

"It sounds like you are part of that 47% who could be qualified as a Kinsey zero and don't have any attraction to the same sex."

I pressed further, "So if you do not see the possibility of re-orientating yourself, then why would you presume that John can make that jump?"

He shrugged, "I'm not sure. This NARTH group, however, was suggesting that being gay worked against our innate human nature and so being gay is changeable. They seem to suggest that there are no gay people, just straight people with gay behaviors."

I expounded, "Right. More specifically, they argue that the gay condition is a matter of environment and nurturing, rather than an unchangeable biological condition. And second, as a result, it is simply a condition that is changeable with therapy."

Conversion Therapy...Can You Fix 'Gay?'

"Yes, that is what I got out of it. What do you think of that position?" he asked.

"I think that most in the mental health field, including conservative Christian practitioners, would agree that the development of sexual orientation is more complicated than just nature vs. nurture. I have not come across many responsible mental health clinicians who would argue that it was strictly one or the other. Even NARTH notes that there are biological influences in these stages of development," I explained.

I continued, "I think the disagreement happens over whether the gay orientation is one that can or should be fixed. NARTH would say that for those who want to change it is possible and should be encouraged since being gay is, in their perspective, not healthy."

"Right, they believe that people can change their orientation if they want to," he said.

Over Coffee

"Did John want to?"

"He originally wanted to. But he says he already tried for a number of years."

"How did he try?" I inquired.

"He completed a program in and counseled with a mental health specialist in reparative therapy."

"Was he successful?"

"He claims that it didn't help him at all. He said he was only able to suppress his thoughts a bit, but that he still wasn't able to ever be attracted to a woman. Evidently they encouraged him to date women, in combination with developing relationships with straight guys he was attracted to. As he put it,"

Conversion Therapy...Can You Fix 'Gay?'

I found a great looking Christian gal to date. Most of my straight friends were jealous.

I tried to make it work and made a real effort. Still, she decided to break it off. She told me that she was too frustrated since I didn't seem attracted to her. Then I got the 'let's be friends' brush-off.

I decided to tell her about the therapy I was in.

She was remarkably unshaken by my confession, saying, 'Well I hope you don't mind if I tell you this, but it is obvious that you are not remotely aroused by me. I don't really understand why you are trying to force yourself to do something you aren't going to be able to do. And any guy you find would be lucky to have you.'

Over Coffee

Then she added, 'But it's not fair for either of us for you to be dishonest about the fact that you are not ever going to be aroused by me. I need that. It's part of a healthy relationship.'

It really hit me that I was being selfish and that I was not doing anything but hurting people by trying to force myself to be attracted to women when I simply never would be. I told her how grateful I was for her honesty. I am glad that we are still friends.

As far as developing straight friends, I already had them. And some of them were guys I found attractive. It still didn't change the fact that I couldn't have been less interested in girls, and more interested in finding another gay man who was like my straight friends, but was gay. I finally found all of those qualities in this Christian guy I told you about.

Conversion Therapy...Can You Fix 'Gay?'

"It sounds like John is at least a Kinsey five," I concluded.

"Why is that important?"

"I think the main difference for a Kinsey five or six is that there is only one orientation to favor. Other people possess some amount of both orientations. So for them it's more a matter of learning how to repress one in favor of the other that is already available. They can foster either orientation if they choose to."

"What do you mean?"

"In others words, for a strictly gay person there is only the gay orientation to favor. And for the strictly straight person there is only the straight orientation to favor. For all the others who possess both, they are able to foster an orientation which is already present, toward one or both orientations."

Over Coffee

The pastor paused in reflection, then asked, "So you think that someone who is in the middle of the Kinsey Scale, who possesses an orientation to both sexes can and should choose a heterosexual orientation?"

It was a good question, and a difficult one. I paused for a moment to consider, then remarked, "In the case of a truly middle-of-the-road Kinsey three or four I would probably say it would be the biblical suggestion."

I continued, "However, in my experience, there is far more to consider. Circumstances don't always make it so simple. Sometimes it can be difficult for this small group of people, especially in the church, to discover what their orientation actually is. Often they have never been provided with the ability to consider that they may be gay."

The pastor looked confused, asking, "I'm not sure I follow."

Conversion Therapy...Can You Fix 'Gay?'

I reflected, "I have talked with a number of gay-questioning individuals who have grown up in the church; some orthodox, some protestant, and some catholic. For many of these people it can be difficult to consider themselves as actually being gay. In many cases, because they don't identify with the gay lifestyle as it is often portrayed, they don't consider that they could be gay. They have in fact never actually been aroused by the opposite sex, moreover they hide the fact that they are aroused by the same sex. Often they can be under the perception that there is some magical person of the opposite sex out there who will flip that switch for them. They may be able to identify what is attractive in the opposite sex, but still never have any *sexual* attraction toward them. In these cases, many of these people define themselves as having both orientations largely because they fear considering themselves as gay."

I continued, "In many cases, these people will continue dating the opposite sex, because that is what their church or society expects of them."

Over Coffee

The pastor added, "So you think that some people need to take the time to actually figure out what their orientation is?"

"That is possible," I replied. "Just like John, it took him a while to realize that he was never going to be able to be attracted to a woman."

The pastor interjected, "You know... John mentioned that he first considered himself straight even though he had never actually been attracted to a woman. Later, he held on to being bisexual for a while till he finally came to the conclusion after his therapy that he wasn't going to be able to change. That was sort of confusing to me at first, but I can see where he was coming from now."

Puberty? Again?!

The pastor took a bite of his pastry and sat back for a few seconds. I went to work on my pastry and welcomed a quick break. Finally the pastor brought the conversation back, noting, "As far as

Conversion Therapy...Can You Fix 'Gay?'

I understand it, NARTH seems to think that gay people can create an orientation to the opposite sex by helping them to identify with their own gender and fulfill their need for intimacy with their same gender. And that eventually this will provide the opportunity for an unfamiliarity with the opposite gender and therefore an attraction, just like it happened with them when they were younger."

"I think you hit the nail right on the head, there."

"How so?" he asked, puzzled.

"I mean, when you said, 'just like it happened with them when they were younger.'"

"I don't follow."

"Well, reparative therapy is essentially trying to re-create the same situation a person experienced in pre-pubescence, or before puberty hit."

Over Coffee

"What do you mean?"

"Here's an example. For a boy, they would say that sexual orientation develops as a result of his early identification with other boys; his own gender. In contrast, he finds girls as strange and curious. Then when puberty hits, this curiosity is driven by the hormonal influences, causing the boy to be attracted to girls."

The pastor nodded. "Right, that is sort of what I got from their material. And they would suggest that for a gay man, he never was able to identify with other boys, but instead identified with other girls. And since he found boys as strange and curious, his hormones drove his curiosity into an attraction to other boys, rather than girls."

"Precisely," I agreed.

"But that sounds pretty strong to me," he surmised.

Conversion Therapy...Can You Fix 'Gay?'

"I think that it is worthy of consideration, although it's sort of a 'chicken or the egg' situation. Was it a genetic disposition that caused the boy to identify less with his own gender, eventually leading him to a gay attraction? Or was it some other sort of environmental cause?"

"Tough to say, I suppose," he admitted.

"I agree," I said, adding, "Additionally, I think we can safely say, whether it was genetic or environmental, the reality is that sexual orientation happens to a person. It's not a ballot with a gay/straight option that they check off."

The pastor chuckled, saying, "No, I don't suppose it is. Otherwise I imagine most gay people probably would have initially voted to be straight."

He shifted in his seat and asked, "So, I guess their reparative therapy works then. You should be able to help a guy become familiar with the guys he is curious about or attracted to, and that will allow him to develop his unfamiliarity and attraction to women."

"Well, that certainly is the thought. But did it work for John?" I queried.

"According to him it didn't have any real effect in creating an attraction to women at all."

"And in point of fact, even NARTH notes that a handful of their cases are unable to be successful in that. I would imagine John is one of those."

"But why?" he asked.

"Well, I'm certainly not a clinical specialist, or a licensed mental health counselor, but I can't help but see a huge missing element in their equation."

Taken aback he asked, "What's that?"

Conversion Therapy...Can You Fix 'Gay?'

"What about puberty?"

He blinked. "What about it?"

"Well, how many times does it happen in a person's life?"

"Just once, thank goodness," he laughed.

"That's exactly my point. They are missing the puberty part of the equation. They are asking gay people to somehow reproduce a biologically hard-wired and physical/chemical, one-time altering event in their life. Unfortunately, you just cannot recreate puberty."

"Again, thank goodness." He breathed a sigh of relief.

"So all of the regression therapy that goes into creating a 'healthy' pre-puberty familiarity with their own gender still won't reproduce the event of puberty."

"I suppose not. There's no changing the hard-wires," he agreed, smiling.

Conversion or Suppression?

I extended my thought. "In fact, I think that conversion, or reparative therapy is probably not the best name for what is happening in the case of their successful people. It is actually more about suppression therapy."

"Why suppression therapy?" he asked.

"Because someone who is successful in their program is not really creating an orientation that wasn't already hardwired by puberty. They are actually just suppressing one orientation for the other which is available to them. But in the case of a Kinsey five or six, they are suppressing sexuality com-

Conversion Therapy...Can You Fix 'Gay?'

pletely, since there is no other orientation there to begin with."

"So what's the problem?" he asked.

"In the end, the problem is that for the Kinsey five or six people like John, suppression therapy does not provide any remedy or outlet for their God-intended need for companionship and intimacy. In fact, what it does provide for is opportunity for promiscuity, depression, anxiety and a number of other harmful consequences since this innate and God-intended human need is going unmet."

The pastor reflected on what I said for a couple moments, scratching his arm a bit. "It seems pretty frustrating to me that NARTH wouldn't acknowledge the Kinsey Scale and the reality that there are people who might only possess a gay orientation."

I nodded, adding, "I suppose that is what shocked me most about NARTH's available literature, and even Dr. Joseph Nicholosi's works on the matter, their "change guru". There was a complete absence of conversation concerning such a significant work as Kinsey's study.

The pastor shrugged his shoulders saying, "So it sounds as if you are arguing that there is no point in recommending reparative therapy for gay people."

I interjected, "I'm not the only one. Exodus International, one of the leading conversion programs for biblical faith churches recently announced that they are no longer using reparative therapy. They concluded that it is not effective. In point of fact, the organization itself dreid up for lack of support and effectiveness."

The pastor raised his eyebrows, astonished, "Are you kidding me?! What about the thousands of Christians men and women like John who underwent years of this therapy? That's a tragedy."

I sighed a bit. "I agree. I personally know many people who left the Church because they alledgedly failed in their therapy. In reality they were set up for failure."

The pastor stabbed his empty plate, "That's an absolute tragedy. God forgive us."

Over Coffee

Chapter 5

What About the Bible?

Over Coffee

I dug into the last morsel of my Ham. It was pretty darn tasty to say the least. Cleaning up the last of the hashbrowns from my plate, I pushed it aside and pulled in my coffee for a couple of sips.

The pastor took a deep breath; the kind one takes to mark an emphasis to their coming phrase. He placed both hands on the table and said with a hint of hesitancy, "So now comes the obvious question of the biblical passages."

"Obvious?" I asked, raising one eyebrow.

"I thought you said you weren't going to be one of those..." he began with a mix of irritation and nervous jesting.

I interjected humorously, "...those liberals who ask you to not take the scriptures so literally?"

What About the Bible?

"Well, you said it, not me," he said shrugging his shoulders and adding, "I was going to cry 'bait & switch.'"

I laughed, "No, I believe that God inspired the authors of Scripture and they meant what they wrote."

The pastor's shoulders relaxed a bit. He moved forward in his seat and leaned in saying, "I realize that I am pretty conservative when it comes to my interpretation of Scripture. So I'm not going to be able to dismiss parts of the Scripture simply because they make for bad press. But I understand that I need to be responsible with my interpretation and hermeneutic."

"Whoa... hermeneutic?" I questioned sarcastically.

"Big words, eh, for a small town pastor?" he added.

Over Coffee

"You said it, not me," I playfully jabbed.

"But seriously, what do you do with the verses that so explicitly forbid homosexual acts?" he inquired.

"Ah, the 'clobber' passages," I noted.

"The what?" he questioned, taken aback.

"The clobber passages. At least, that is what many in the gay community call them."

He laughed. "I've never heard that. But I can understand why they gave them that name." He continued, "So what do you do with the clobber passages?"

"Absolutely nothing. That's what I do," I said with an intentional hint of nonchalance.

What About the Bible?

The pastor looked at me with a befuddled stare, trying to decide what he was supposed to do with the unexpected statement. He hung there, awaiting my cue, hinting with a quick lean forward that he was stalling for the punch-line.

After a few puzzled seconds, he said, "Are you serious?" and fell back in his seat, confused.

"That wasn't exactly what I was expecting to hear," he said as he pushed his plate to the side in a small display of disappointment.

"You weren't expecting that?" I asked, recognizing his frustration.

"Well frankly, no. I was expecting some sort of decent argument," he said, somewhere between humor and dismay.

"Well, if I must," I jibed.

Over Coffee

"Ah hah! Here it comes!" he exclaimed, shaking his head.

I laughed and took a sip of coffee.

Literally Speaking

"Like I said earlier, I am not asking anyone to forsake the inspiration of Scripture. I believe God inspired the authors to write the words that they did. And I am not asking anyone to suggest that the Scripture is erroneous in any way."

I continued, "I'm not going to delve into much argumentation around the issue, largely because I don't think it is crucial to the issue. I think that there is room to converse concerning the translation of some passages. Anyone who has spent any time working with the original biblical languages, Hebrew and Greek, would have to agree that the words are not always easy to translate. They are not always crystal clear. Just because someone waves a magic wand over a translation and publishes it in

What About the Bible?

a leather binding does not mean that it is a perfect translation."

Holding my hand to my chest, I clarified. "But let me be emphatically clear on this matter. I am not saying that the original authors were incorrect! I *am* saying, however, that the translation into the English has at times been very one-sided on the gay issue."

"Even so, in my view it does not change the reality, as I stated before, that sexuality initially came as a result of God's separation of His creature into their respective and equal genders, with the intention of them being joined back together as one flesh."

God's Law vs God's Intention

I continued, "I think it would be hard to argue that God creatively intended people to be sexually oriented to the same gender. It seems a bit counterintuitive to build a creature that is procreatively aroused by a gender that does not yield the ability to procreate."

"Hmm...you are hardly building a strong case for gay partnership here," he noted, rubbing the back of his neck.

"But the problem is that we aren't living in the Garden of Eden. The Garden is gone. Now the once idealistic soil yields uncertainty, complexity and chaos. Not one of us as humans enjoy the luxury of innocence nor perfection. Instead we have to face the realities of injury, current human genetics, hurt and consequence." I continued, "But that's not the end of it, is it?"

"What do you mean?" he asked.

"I mean, there's a big difference between what God started in the Garden, and what His plan was for the end of time. Sure, Adam and Eve were created to be one flesh and commanded to be 'fruitful and multiply.' But after the proverbial apple was bitten, we are no longer talking about the Garden-state, we are talking about a world of chaos."

"I presume you are not throwing the baby out with the bath water. We do after all have to have some standards," the pastor stated emphatically.

I nodded quickly in agreement adding, "Of course. That is what God's law was meant for. But the reality is that people are sometimes unable to fulfill the perfection of God's laws due to circumstances outside of their control. Sometimes, the ideal situation is to allow people to live a life they are capable of. Oftentimes that life is more fulfilling of the *intention* of God's laws and is more godly than the situation in which they are currently living."

Priorities

I was curious to hear the pastor's thoughts, so I asked "I'd actually prefer to hear your thoughts on those passages."

Over Coffee

He took a sip of his coffee. Then shrugged his shoulders, pursing his mouth to one side. "I'll be upfront with you. I really don't know what to do with them. After all it is a pretty clear commandment that a man should not sleep with another man."

"Commandment?" I asked.

"Yeah."

"It certainly is on the Levitical law list, equally and alongside adultery, and cursing a parent. But does God consider it substantial enough to include it in the Ten Commandments?"

"Well..." he trailed off.

"And Jesus is never noted as saying anything remotely touching the subject, however, he does spend a considerable amount of time talking about adultery, divorce and remarriage, right?"

What About the Bible?

"But there are still verses talking about it," he stated confidently.

"Well, certainly, but let's be sure to give them their proper focus and attention."

"So you think that some commandments are more important that others?" he asked, perplexed.

"No, but I think that there are some commandments that are higher on the priority list depending on the situation at hand. And we often treat them with a level of priority. Let's consider the Commandment, 'Remember the Sabbath and keep it holy.'"

"OK," he said warily.

"When was the last time you stoned someone in your congregation for taking an extra shift at work on the Sabbath?"

Over Coffee

"Well that's pretty extreme," he replied, cocking his head to the side.

"True. But doesn't God state, in Exodus 31:15, "For six days, work is to be done, but the seventh day is a Sabbath of rest, holy to the LORD. Whoever does any work on the Sabbath day must be put to death?"

"Yes, but some of my people have to work when they are told so they can keep their job. They have to survive," he noted.

"That's very much my point," I noted, continuing, "So let's back it up a bit. When was the last time you even bothered forbidding your congregation from doing any work on the Sabbath?"

"That's probably the last thing on my list right now. I'm too busy trying to help people not cheat on their spouses, not spend their paychecks on gambling, or helping couples reconcile themselves

What About the Bible?

after one has become physically abusive," he admitted.

"Right!" I exclaimed. "And I presume that you don't deny membership to people who have jobs that require them to work on the Sabbath?"

"No." he confirmed. "In fact I have fellow pastors who have to hold down an extra job to support themselves, which requires them to work on an occasional Sunday."

Commands, Context, and Conflict

The pastor asserted, "But for me, the Bible seems to clearly say that a man should not sleep with another man. That seems pretty straightforward." He paused waiting for a response.

I continued, "If we are talking about clear commandments, let's go back again to the Sabbath. God is even more straightforward about that than a man sleeping with another man. The Scripture states:"

> Whoever does any work on the Sabbath day must be put to death...
>
> - Exodus 35:15 NIV

I added, "In fact, the death sentence for working on the Sabbath is mentioned more often than our perceived anti-gay passage, which isn't even on the top-ten. If that's not clear enough, in the book of Numbers, the Scriptures record the actual stoning of a man who collected wood on the Sabbath."

The pastor nodded his head and added, "Yes, but in the New Testament Jesus healed a man on the Sabbath and said:"

> ...it is lawful to do good on the Sabbath.

What About the Bible?

- Matthew 12:12 NIV

I reflected, "Well, sure...*healing* certainly qualifies as *good*. But do you allow people in your congregation to *work* on the Sabbath?"

He contested, "I'm not going to stone anyone in our congregation for doing their job on the Sabbath. Like I was saying, there are a handful of people who don't have any choice in the matter. Their job may at times require them to work for ten days straight, after which they have a few days off. It is good for them to have income to pay their bills. Sure, they aren't able to follow the same seven-day schedule of the commandment, but they still have some days off. In the end they are fulfilling the intent of the commandment, even if it isn't perfect."

I happily agreed, "But that's exactly my point."

"What is?" he asked.

Over Coffee

"They aren't able to fulfill the perfection of the commandment because of their context. Still, it is good for them to pay their bills. In other words, the context of their job puts them in a place where they have to choose between the good of the commandment, and the good of their own survival," I replied.

The pastor interjected, "Well, their situation is pretty unique."

"I totally agree. And in the case of the Kinsey five or six, their situation, or context is very unique. John is in a situation where he is also asked to choose between the good of two commandments. He must choose between God's commandment for a man not to sleep with another man, and God's commandment, that man should not be alone. God created humans to need someone and John needs companionship."

The pastor asked, confused, "I'm not sure what you mean by God's commandment that man should not be alone."

What About the Bible?

"It is the first commandment, the first moral rule God established regarding man. It's a rule He set for Himself: It is not good for man to be alone."

"So you're saying that it is a sin for man to be alone?" he asked.

"I would say that it is wrong to force someone into isolation when they have no desire for it. We do this in prisons, calling it solitary confinement. It is viewed as a punishment. And the reason it is so effective is because we were not intended to be forced into isolation."

"Yes. I suppose that is true," he begrudgingly agreed.

"But isn't that what the Church is requiring for people like John?" I asked.

"Yes and no. God created Eve so that man wouldn't be alone."

Over Coffee

I countered, "True, but we are talking about a context where a man, or for that matter a woman, is not able to have that type of relationship. By whatever means John came to his orientation, it doesn't change the fact that he is incapable of being attracted to a woman. So our churches are in fact forcing John into isolation since we are giving him no other option."

Chapter 6

Jesus and Human Ability

Over Coffee

The pastor contemplated this for a moment and then began again. "But I know that the moment I go to my board with this they are going to say that even if we can demonstrate John is not able to change, and doesn't want to be celibate, we cannot encourage him to 'live in sin.'"

Patiently, I asked, "Can we return to the passage in Matthew, Chapter 19?"

"Right, the one on divorce and remarriage," he said dropping his tone with a bit of a sigh, as if acknowledging that this was a passage he was very familiar with.

"Exactly."

I hesitated for a second, noticing that the pastor's demeanor had changed a bit. I leaned forward inquisitively, saying, "You sound like you have had to deal with this passage lately."

"It was a recent decision by our church board. They allowed a couple to maintain their membership after they were divorced and remarried."

"What were the circumstances, if I may ask?"

"Well, I'm telling you about a gay guy in my congregation. I might as well be transparent about straight dilemmas," he laughed, attempting to bring levity to the conversation.

"So what was the hang-up?" I asked.

The pastor pushed back his sleeves a bit and began. "We already have couples in our church who are divorced and remarried. Both of them were cases where their spouse had committed some sort of infidelity, so there wasn't any scriptural problem with their divorce and remarriage."

Over Coffee

"I presume that is because Jesus provides the exception of divorce and remarriage in the case of infidelity?" I asked.

"Right. At least, that was the means by which we were able to reconcile their situation."

He continued, "But in this new case, there was no infidelity. The wife divorced her husband, a member of the Board at the time, because he was beating her. The husband, refusing to reconcile his abuse or deal with the issue, resigned from the Board and ended up leaving the church, moving out of state. The members, however, voted to continue the wife's membership in the church."

"She found a man in the church, who had not been married. The both of them wanted to be married and approached me to conduct the wedding. One of the Board members was concerned that it was not appropriate for me to conduct the ceremony, since her divorce was not due to infidelity."

Jesus and Human Ability

I asked, "Did the Board allow you to conduct the ceremony and allow them to continue their membership as a remarried couple?"

"Yes, for which I am very glad. They both are wonderful, generous, and humble people," he said with a look of fond recollection.

"Interesting," I mumbled.

"What?" he said raising his eyebrows, "I've often found 'interesting' to mean 'I have a strong opinion on that.'"

"So you've allowed a relaxing of God's law in order to curb against a worse situation."

"How is that relaxing God's law?"

"Well, according to Jesus,"

Over Coffee

> I tell you that anyone who divorces his wife, except for marital unfaithfulness, and marries another woman commits adultery.
>
> - Matthew 19:9 NIV

"Despite Jesus's statement, you permitted her to not only separate but to also remarry, even when her original divorce was not in the case of infidelity."

Matter-of-factly he stated, "Well, we certainly were not going to force her to stay in a marriage where the husband was beating her. After that, we could not force her to be alone the rest of her life. That would hardly be a healthy situation, and I doubt she would stay in the church for long since she would eventually want to be with someone."

I chimed in, "I totally agree. I'm sure that John would agree too. No doubt he would sympathize with her predicament."

"But it's different; he's gay," the pastor argued.

"Is it? Both are a relaxing of God's law in some manner. In the case of this woman, you are allowing her to live in a situation that is scripturally adulterous. In fact, even the other divorced and remarried people are technically living in imperfect situations where God's law is concerned."

"But the others had infidelity in their previous relationships. And Jesus provides an exception for infidelity," he contested.

"Exactly!"

"I'm not following," he remarked shaking his head.

I clarified, "Just before that exception doesn't Jesus state that 'what God has brought together, let no man separate?'"

Over Coffee

"Yes."

"So," I continued, "is Jesus, speaking as God, contradicting himself by stating that people should not separate, and then turning around and saying they should?"

"Well, I would hardly say that God would contradict Himself," he stated obviously.

"OK, so then Jesus is more likely saying, 'God's law is that no marriages should be separated, but in the case of adultery, a situation has been created where the law as it is written may no longer fulfill God's intention behind that law.'"

The pastor tapped his finger on an imaginary spot on the table, stating, "That's the way we saw it, in the case of our recent remarriage. We recognize that the ideal is marriage, but in the case of the husband's physical abuse, that situation was no longer ideal. And then when she wanted to be married again, it seemed loving to allow her to marry another Christian man rather than force her into isolation."

"So you allowed her to live in a situation that did not meet the perfection of the law, but *did* fulfill the intention of the law. As a result she could live in a situation that was actually within her ability and better than her current situation?" I asked.

"Right," he concurred.

Gay Partnership: a Human Ability

"I think I see where you are going with this," the pastor added. He continued, "So you are suggesting that John should be allowed to live in a partnership with this other gay Christian guy, because it fulfills the intention of God's law—that we should not be alone—in a way that he is capable of."

"Precisely!" I exclaimed, almost spilling my coffee. "That's exactly it!"

Over Coffee

"But wouldn't we be encouraging them to live in sin?"

"I suppose that was the very question you raised with this recently married couple."

"Yes, it was," he acknowledged.

"So did you conclude that this woman and her new husband would be living in sin?" I asked.

"We concluded that they were going to be better able to live a godly life in their marriage than they would if they were forced to live in isolation. I'm guessing that is probably what you would argue for John," he stated in an attempt to beat me to the punch.

"May I ask another question?" I inquired.

"Sure." He took another sip of coffee.

"Which one of us in this life is ever able to say that we are not living in sin?"

The pastor quickly noted, "Well I'm not living in sin."

"Well, bless my soul...I'm sitting with a perfect man," I gently mocked.

The pastor cocked his head off to one side, furrowing his eyebrows in a display of dissatisfaction with my remark. "I think in this case you are being a bit loosey-goosey with the word sin," he stated, obviously feeling exasperated.

"Why is that?"

"Well, I'm certainly far from perfection, but I do my best within my ability to live as good a life as I can."

Over Coffee

"But that's my point. You've qualified your perfection by noting your ability. Or to put it another way, you've excused your sin, or imperfections, as being outside of your ability."

I continued, "I don't think anyone would expect me to be perfect, but they would expect me to do the best I am able to do within my ability."

"Well, what else can we do?" he concurred.

"Yet John is unable to be anything but gay. He has demonstrated that it is not within his ability to change his orientation. More than that, he is not going to be able to live as a single person."

"But if you allow that, you are opening the door onto a slippery slope."

"How so?" I asked.

"You'll be opening the door for any person to be partnered."

"Whoa, there!" I said, smiling and holding my hands up. "I could say the same about your remarriage situation, that you are opening the door for anyone to divorce their spouse and remarry - over burnt toast."

The pastor protested, "Just because we are allowing for a unique situation, with a very small percentage, that doesn't mean we are allowing a blanket open door for divorce and remarriage."

"Exactly. Likewise, just because you allow John to live in a committed partnership, it doesn't mean that you are saying that anyone who claims they are gay should randomly partner-up with any other gay person."

I added, "Also, the number of people in our churches that are divorced and remarried probably far outweigh the number of Kinsey fives or sixes, who are Christian, gay persons that are not able to be celibate. Moreover, those who are divorced and remarried in our churches, in many cases, were not divorced due to infidelity in their previous marriages and so are permitted to be members despite their current and potentially adulterous situation."

I continued, "So we are talking about a very small group of people in our congregations who are actually Kinsey fives or sixes, like John, and probably even fewer who additionally wish to be partnered."

Chapter 7

Moving Forward: Obstacle or Opportunity?

Over Coffee

Pat came to the table for a final time noting, "I'm going to have to start charging the two of you rent."

The pastor looked at his watch, reacting with a bit of a shock. "Good grief! I didn't realize we had been here that long. Sorry, Pat."

"Oh, it's no bother to me, Pastor. Besides, you two were looking like you were solving the world's problems and we're not turning people away here, so..." she remarked.

I looked at my watch, discovering we had been talking for a couple of hours, adding my own "Yikes!" to the conversation.

The pastor looked up at Pat, asking her for the check, which she kindly pulled out of her pocket, and placed on the table.

Moving Forward: Obstacle or Opportunity?

The both of us hurriedly reached out to grab the ticket, but the pastor insisted that he do the honors of picking up the tab.

After a few seconds and a couple more sips of coffee he started again, saying, "Well, you've given me a whole lot to think about here, although I'm still not sure what to do with it." Looking down at his coffee cup, he added, "Even if I agreed with you, I'm still not sure how this is going to work in practice. You're asking me to direct the church to accept something that we never have."

The Challenge of the Viewable

I nodded my head in acknowledgement of his frustration, saying, "I have the utmost sympathy for your dilemma. There really is nothing comfortable about compassion. I think the notion of grace is most drastically challenged by those things we are forced to see face to face."

"What do you mean?" he asked.

Over Coffee

"I mean, it is one thing to allow a couple to be married in the congregation who have been divorced. Nobody but God would ever know their situation to look at them. It is another thing altogether to have a gay couple in your congregation, sitting together in the pew. There's no hiding the fact that two men or two women are sitting together. They provide a clear and visible reality of their situation, which they cannot hide."

"Exactly. It sort of sits out there for everyone to see." He paused in reflection, adding, "But is our faith one that promotes grace and acceptance only to those who qualify for it because their humanity lives below the radar of people's vision? That seems like a pretty shallow grace and a very limited love."

I nodded in agreement, adding, "Well, there certainly is nothing comfortable about change, either. Allowing John to sit in the pew with his partner will mean that people will ask questions. Little Suzy is going to probably ask her mom why those two men sit together like her mom and dad do."

Moving Forward: Obstacle or Opportunity?

He sighed in agreement. "That's exactly right. That's where so many people miss the boat when it comes to talking about these things. It seems so simple when you are sitting here in a restaurant or at seminary. But when it comes to the pews, we pastors are left holding the bag."

A New Education

I laughed, noting, "I couldn't agree more. But can I ask you?"

He shrugged, waiting for my question.

I continued, "So what if little Suzy asks her parents about John and his partner? How is that any different than when Suzy asks her mom why another child in her Sunday school class only has one parent? Isn't it just another opportunity for Suzy's mom to talk about the grace and love of Christ and His church? Aren't those the exceptional moments when we have a unique chance to show our children what makes the Church as a community so different from everyone else?"

"But that means education," he noted. "How do I help to provide those answers for parents to give to their children, or other parents, or anyone for that matter? There isn't a lot of literature out there for this sort of thing on the conservative side."

"There is actually quite a bit out there, but yeah, probably not on the conservative side. You may find yourself talking to some liberals after all," I said, smiling.

"Bite your tongue!" he jested.

I smiled, "Or even better, John seems like a capable guy. Why not put him in charge of a committee for the purpose of educating the congregation?" I suggested and continued, "Pastor, if I may, having talked to a number of people in some very conservative churches, your situation is not uncommon. There are a number of people who are find-

Moving Forward: Obstacle or Opportunity?

ing ways to work this issue out in their congregations. I am certain that working together on the matter will provide a tremendous amount of resources."

"No, I think you are right about that. I suspect there are a number of people who would step up to the plate and would welcome the change," he reflected.

Over Coffee

Chapter 8
Friendly Goodbyes

Over Coffee

The pastor smiled, and leaning forward said, "I think I'm about as torn as a man can be. On the one hand I have a church and denomination who are shored up against the idea of permitting gay partnership. And on the other hand I have my heart and mind struck with something pretty challenging...," he paused, "and a child of God placed under my keeping who is dear to my heart."

I replied, "Pastor, I do not envy you. You are a man who is honest and compassionate, and I'm afraid those are undervalued qualities at times. Thank you for hearing my thoughts and thank you for not taking John's situation lightly."

He nodded his head in appreciation, lifting his arm out from the table, saying "Shall we?"

We gathered ourselves up and prepared to face the falling rain outside, making our way through the cafe to the door. The pastor waved a friendly

Friendly Goodbyes

goodbye to Pat who shouted back, "You boys stay dry now!"

Once again we stood on the covered porch outside the Old Milwaukee Cafe. The pastor zipped up his coat and let out a shiver. Placing his hands in his pockets and staring out onto the street before us he remarked, "I can't say that I'm ready to take your argument hook, line, and sinker, Dave," he paused, then added, "But I can't say that I am certain either way anymore."

I stood there to the left of him in silence for a few moments, acknowledging his candor with a couple of nods. Grateful for his honesty, I replied, "Pastor, thank you for being open to the conversation and thank you for the coffee. I hope your congregation knows how lucky they are."

The pastor put his arm over my shoulder, saying, "You'll be in my prayers. I'm not going to sugar-coat it, Dave; you have a steep mountain to climb. But I'm going to pray that others will see

Over Coffee

the grace that you are trying to extend to all of our brothers and sisters."

I shook the pastor's hand ending, "Pastor, for you I will pray the same."

About the Author

Over Coffee

Rev. Dave Thompson is the co-founder of World Uniting, Intl' a non-profit whose mission is to promote peace by providing story-based programs that facilitate empathy in order to learn how to love others. Rev. Dave is also the best selling author of *Over Coffee* and the host of OverCoffee.TV, a weekly Sunday morning variety show where Rev. Dave Thompson listens to the spiritual stories of his guests. The show includes open mic peformances from various artists.

Contact Info

Over Coffee

For information about Rev. Dave Thompson, or to book him for speaking engagements, please visit:

overcoffee.tv

If your book club of ten or more would like to Skype with Rev. Dave Thompson free of charge, please contact:

info@worlduniting.org

CPSIA information can be obtained
at www.ICGtesting.com
Printed in the USA
BVHW041734120620
581231BV00007B/296